Fingerpower® Level Four

Effective Technic for All Piano Methods

By John W. Schaum
Edited by Wesley Schaum

FOREWORD

Strong fingers are an important requirement for all pianists, amateur and professional. Schaum Fingerpower® exercises are designed to strengthen all five fingers of both hands. Equal hand developement is assured by the performance of the same patterns in each hand, either in parallel motion or with alternating hands.

The exercises are purposely short and easily memorized. This enables the student to focus his/her efforts on the technical benefits, attentive listening and to playing with a steady beat.

The exercises become progressively more difficult as the student moves through the book. This makes them an ideal companion to a method book at the same level. The exercises are brief and condensed, so they will easily fit in with a student's other musical assignments. There are opportunities for phrase development, rhythmic variety and different types of touch.

The series consists of seven books, Primer Level through Level 6.

PRACTICE SUGGESTIONS

To derive the full benefit from these exercises, they should be played with a firm, solid finger action. **Listen carefully while practicing**. Try to play **each finger equally loud**. Each hand should also play equally loud. It is also important to be aware of the feeling in your fingers and hands during practice.

Each exercise should be practiced four or five times daily, starting at a slow tempo and gradually increasing the tempo as proficiency improves. Several previously learned exercises should be reviewed each week as part of regular practice.

ISBN 978-1-936098-28-6

Schaum

EXCLUSIVELY DISTRIBUTED BY

HAL•LEONARD®

Visit Hal Leonard Online at
www.halleonard.com

Contact us:
Hal Leonard
7777 West Bluemound Road
Milwaukee, WI 53213
Email: info@halleonard.com

In Europe, contact:
Hal Leonard Europe Limited
42 Wigmore Street
Marylebone, London, W1U 2RN
Email: info@halleonardeurope.com

In Australia, contact:
Hal Leonard Australia Pty. Ltd.
4 Lentara Court
Cheltenham, Victoria, 3192 Australia
Email: info@halleonard.com.au

CONTENTS - Level Four

Exercise	Page
1. Legato Interval Etude	3
2. Tremolo (Wrist Rotation)	4
3. Rhythmic Wrist Staccato	5
4. Arpeggios in Contrary Motion	6
5. Scales in Contrary Motion	7
6. Thumb Passages	8
7. Wide Range Finger Etude	9
8. Two-Octave Arpeggios (Right Hand)	10
9. Two-Octave Arpeggios (Left Hand)	11
10. Arpeggios in Triplets	12
11. Sustained Thirds	13
12. Major Triad Inversions	14
13. Arpeggio Inversions	15
14. Trills in Thirds	16
15. Triplet Trills	17
16. Double Grace Notes	18
17. Chromatic Hand Contractions	19
18. Finger Expansion	20
19. Equalization of the Fingers	21
20. Four-Finger Dexterity	22
21. Legato Triads and Thirds	23

1. Legato Interval Etude

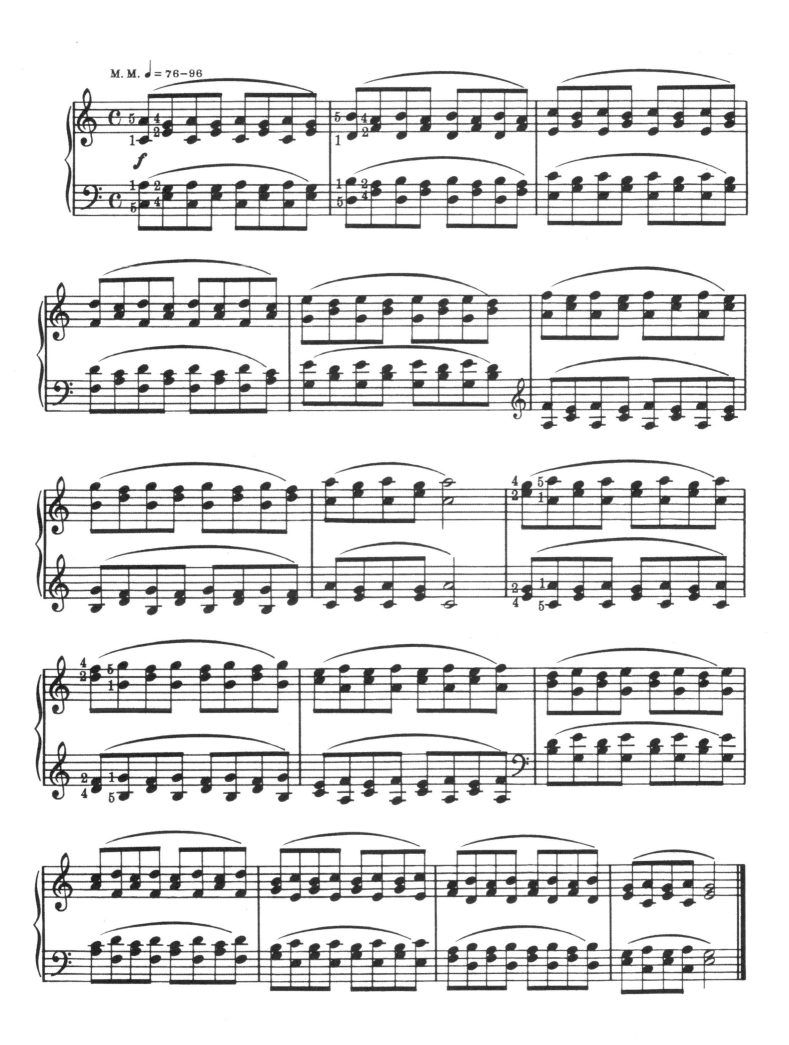

2. Tremolo

(Wrist Rotation)

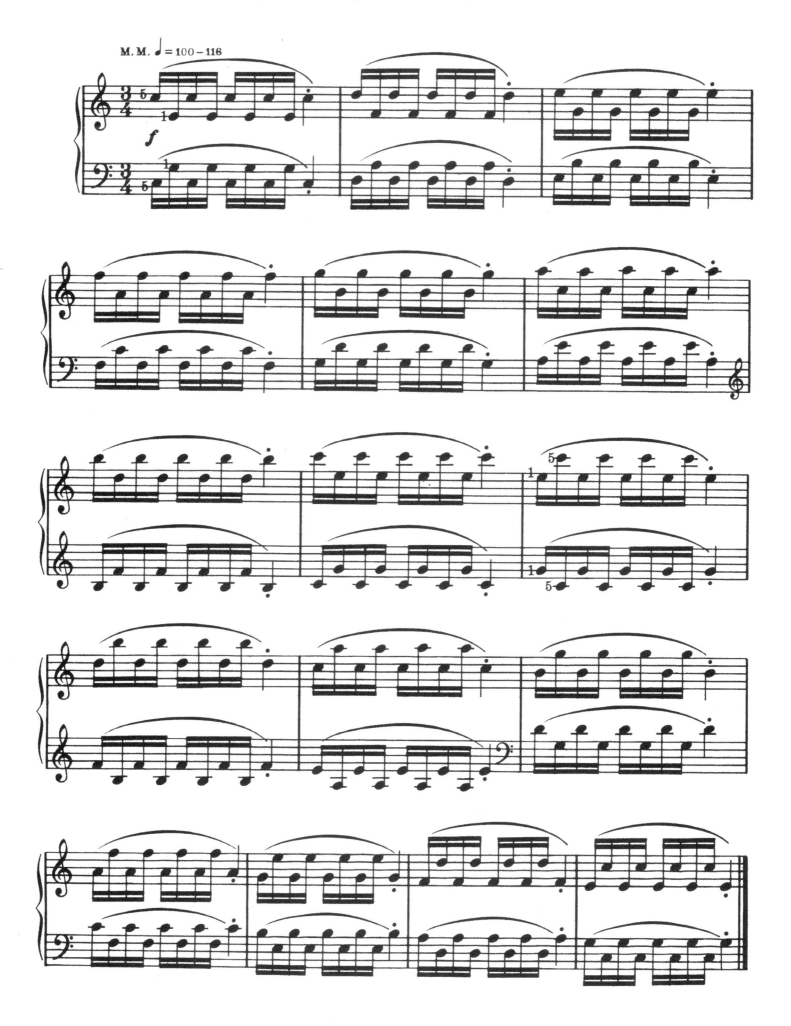

3. Rhythmic Wrist Staccato

4. Arpeggios in Contrary Motion

5. Scales in Contrary Motion

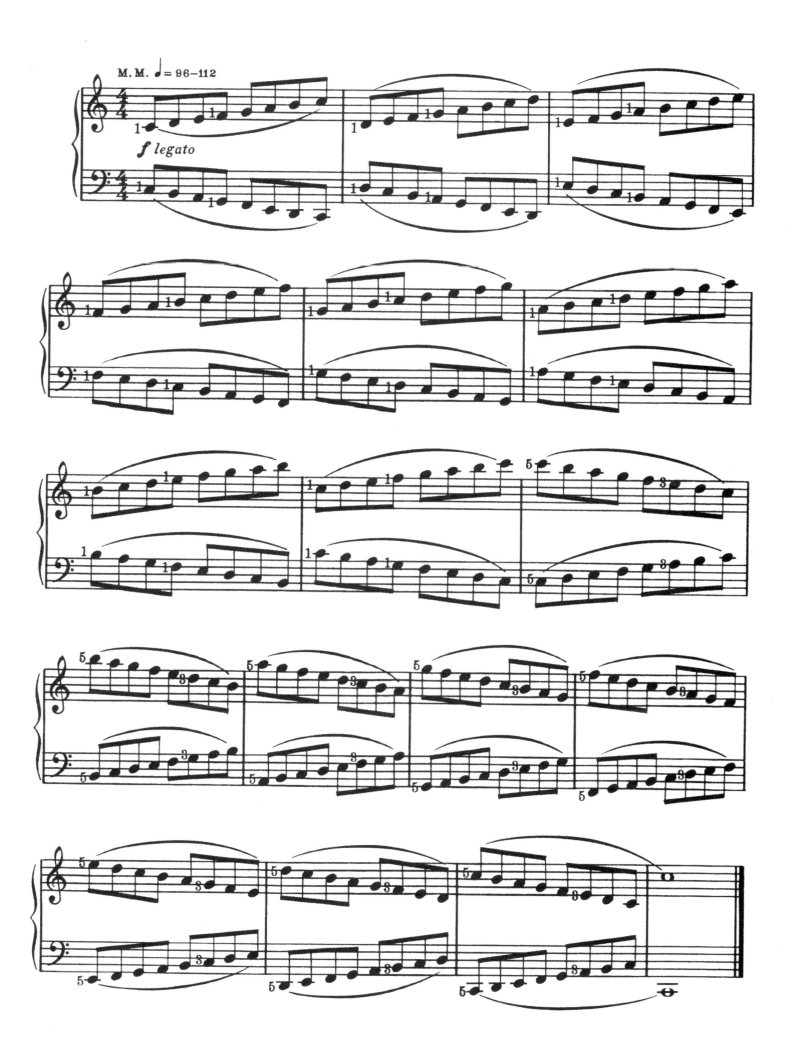

6. Thumb Passages

DIRECTIONS: Also play this study in the following patterns:

{ R.H. 1 – 3 – 1 – 3 – 1 – 3   { R.H. 1 – 4 – 1 – 4 – 1 – 4

{ L.H. 1 – 3 – 1 – 3 – 1 – 3   { L.H. 1 – 4 – 1 – 4 – 1 – 4

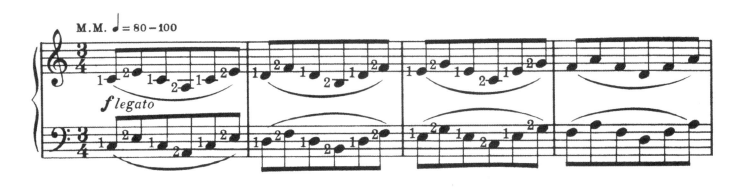

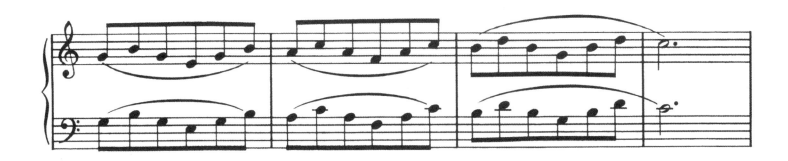

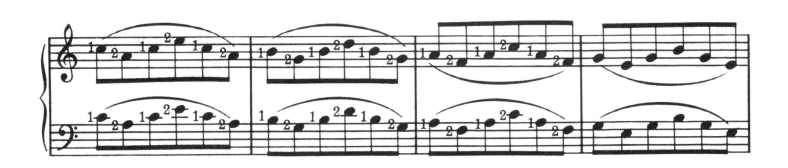

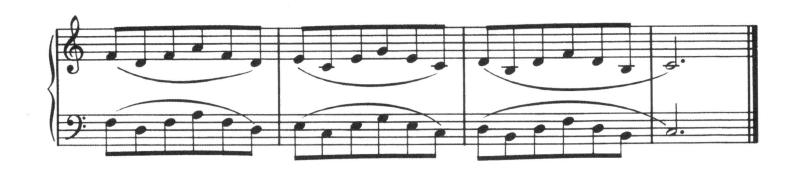

7. Wide Range Finger Etude

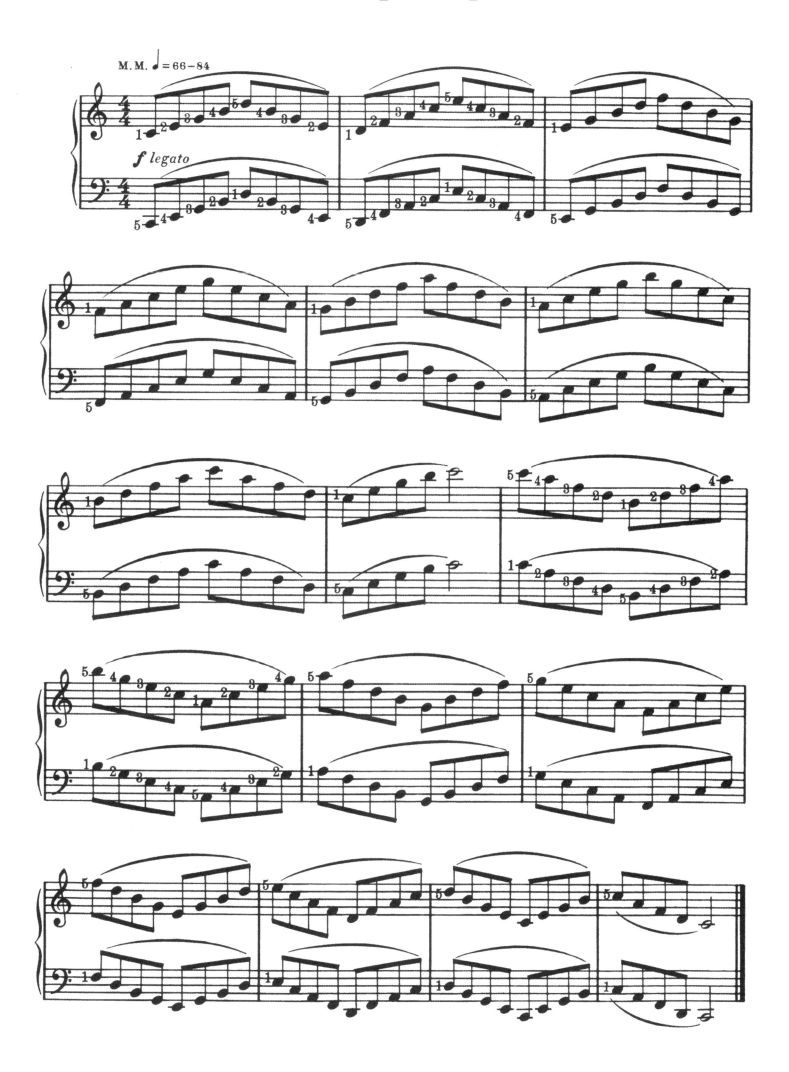

8. Two-Octave Arpeggios

(Right Hand)

9. Two-Octave Arpeggios

(Left Hand)

PREPARATORY DRILL

Play strictly legato

Use same fingering

M. M. ♩ = 100—126

10. Arpeggios in Triplets

11. Sustained Thirds

Note: Play slowly, and strike each finger firmly, the whole note must be strictly held.

M. M. ♩ = 66–88

13

12. Major Triad Inversions

(Ascending and Descending)

13. Arpeggio Inversions

(Ascending and Descending)

14. Trills in Thirds

15. Triplet Trills

16. Double Grace Notes

The quarter notes should be strongly accented.

17. Chromatic Hand Contractions

18. Finger Expansion

The patterns for Etudes numbers 18 and 19 are derived from the diminished seventh chord. Study the following examples.

Dim. 7   Pattern for Etude No. 18   Pattern for Etude No. 19

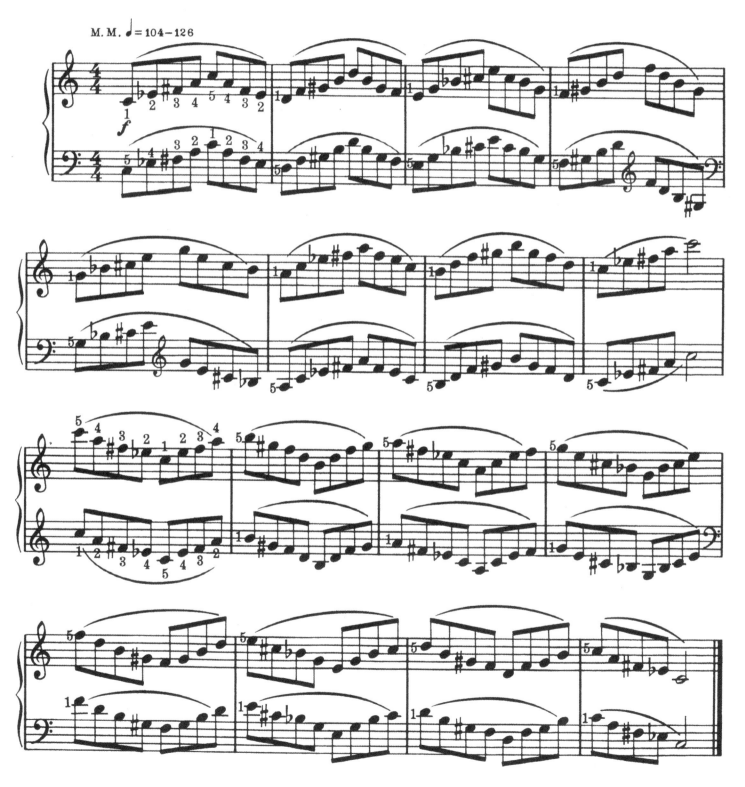

19. Equalization of the Fingers

20. Four-Finger Dexterity

The thumbs are to be omitted throughout this Etude.

21. Legato Triads and Thirds

You are now ready to progress to Schaum **FINGERPOWER**, Level Five.

MORE GREAT SCHAUM PUBLICATIONS

FINGERPOWER®

by John W. Schaum

Physical training and discipline are needed for both athletics and keyboard playing. Keyboard muscle conditioning is called technique. technique exercises are as important to the keyboard player as workouts and calisthenics are to the athlete. Schaum's *Fingerpower®* books are dedicated to development of individual finger strength and dexterity in both hands.

00645334	Primer Level – Book Only	$7.99
00645016	Primer Level – Book/Audio	$9.99
00645335	Level 1 – Book Only	$6.99
00645019	Level 1 – Book/Audio	$8.99
00645336	Level 2 – Book Only	$7.99
00645022	Level 2 – Book/Audio	$9.99
00645337	Level 3 – Book Only	$6.99
00645025	Level 3 – Book/Audio	$7.99
00645338	Level 4 – Book Only	$6.99
00645028	Level 4 – Book/Audio	$9.99
00645339	Level 5 Book Only	$7.99
00645340	Level 6 Book Only	$7.99

FINGERPOWER® ETUDES

Melodic exercises crafted by master technique composers. Modified or transposed etudes provide equal hand development with a planned variety of technical styles, keys, and time signatures.

00645392	Primer Level	$6.99
00645393	Level 1	$6.99
00645394	Level 2	$6.99
00645395	Level 3	$6.99
00645396	Level 4	$6.99

FINGERPOWER® FUN

arr. Wesley Schaum
Early Elementary Level

Musical experiences beyond the traditional *Fingerpower®* books that include fun-to-play pieces with finger exercises and duet accompaniments. Short technique preparatory drills (finger workouts) focus on melodic patterns found in each piece.

00645126	Primer Level	$6.95
00645127	Level 1	$6.99
00645128	Level 2	$6.95
00645129	Level 3	$6.99
00645144	Level 4	$6.95

FINGERPOWER® POP

arr. by James Poteat

10 great pop piano solo arrangements with fun technical warm-ups that complement the *Fingerpower®* series! Can also be used as motivating supplements to any method and in any learning situation.

00237508	Primer Level	$9.99
00237510	Level 1	$9.99
00282865	Level 2	$9.99
00282866	Level 3	$9.99
00282867	Level 4	$10.99

FINGERPOWER® TRANSPOSER

by Wesley Schaum
Early Elementary Level

This book includes 21 short, 8-measure exercises using 5-finger patterns. Positions are based on C,F, and G major and no key signatures are used. Patterns involve intervals of 3rds, 4ths, and 5ths up and down and are transposed from C to F and F to C, C to G and G to C, G to F and F to G.

00645150	Primer Level	$6.95
00645151	Level 1	$6.95
00645152	Level 2	$6.95
00645154	Level 3	$6.95
00645156	Level 4	$6.99

JUMBO STAFF MANUSCRIPT BOOK

This pad features 24 pages with 4 staves per page.

00645936		$4.25

CERTIFICATE OF MUSICAL ACHIEVEMENT

Reward your students for their hard work with these official 8x10-inch certificates that you can customize. 12 per package.

00645938		$6.99

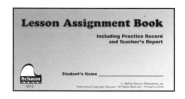

SCHAUM LESSON ASSIGNMENT BOOK

by John Schaum

With space for 32 weeks, this book will help keep students on the right track for their practice time.

00645935		$3.95

HAL•LEONARD®

www.halleonard.com